I0416576

KELVIN SMITH

Stock Market Trading for Teens

This book was professionally typeset on Reedsy.
Find out more at reedsy.com

Contents

Introduction

The stock market is a complex yet fascinating arena where investors engage in buying and selling shares of publicly traded companies. It serves as the primary avenue for businesses to raise capital by offering ownership stakes to investors in the form of stocks. Understanding the stock market entails grasping the intricate dynamics of supply and demand, market trends, and the factors influencing stock prices. This introductory chapter aims to provide a comprehensive overview of the stock market, laying the groundwork for readers to delve deeper into the world of investing.

Understanding Stocks

Stocks, or equities, represent ownership in a corporation and entitle shareholders to a proportional share of the company's assets and earnings. Common stocks, the most prevalent type, grant voting rights in corporate decisions and the potential for dividend payments. On the other hand, preferred stocks often lack voting rights but offer preferential treatment in dividends and asset distribution. Investors analyze various aspects of a company, such as its financial performance, industry outlook, and management team, to assess the potential return and risk associated with owning its stock.

Why Teens Should Learn About the Stock Market

The stock market may seem intimidating to teens at first glance, but its significance in shaping personal finance cannot be overstated. By embarking on a journey to understand the stock market during adolescence, teens lay the groundwork for a lifetime of financial literacy and empowerment. Learning about stocks and investing fosters critical thinking skills, as teens evaluate the merits of different investment opportunities and assess their potential impact on long-term financial goals.

Moreover, early exposure to the stock market cultivates a sense of responsibility and discipline in financial matters. Teens who grasp the concepts of risk management, portfolio diversification, and long-term investing are better equipped to make informed decisions about saving and investing their hard-earned money. This foundational knowledge serves as a springboard for future financial success, enabling teens to navigate the complexities of adulthood with confidence and resilience.

Benefits of Investing at a Young Age

Investing at a young age offers a plethora of advantages that can shape one's financial trajectory for decades to come. Perhaps the most compelling benefit is the power of compounding, wherein investment returns generate additional earnings over time. By starting to invest early, teens harness the full potential of compounding, allowing even modest initial investments to snowball into substantial wealth over the years.

Furthermore, investing at a young age instills valuable lessons in risk management and patience. Teens who weather market fluctuations and resist the temptation to react impulsively to short-term volatility are better positioned to achieve their long-term financial objectives. Additionally, early investors have the luxury of time on their side, affording them the flexibility to pursue higher-risk, higher-reward investment opportunities that may not be suitable for older investors nearing retirement.

In summary, delving into the intricacies of the stock market, understanding the mechanics of stocks, and embracing the art of investing at a young age bestows numerous benefits upon teens. From fostering financial literacy and responsibility to unlocking the power of compounding and long-term wealth accumulation, the journey into the world of investing offers unparalleled opportunities for personal and financial growth.

1

Basics of Investing

Investing is a cornerstone of financial planning and wealth accumulation, encompassing a diverse array of assets and strategies aimed at achieving long-term financial objectives. At its core, investing involves allocating resources, such as money or time, with the expectation of generating a positive return or achieving specific financial goals. Whether it's saving for retirement, funding a child's education, or building a nest egg for the future, understanding the basics of investing is essential for individuals seeking to secure their financial futures and unlock the power of compounding.

Setting Financial Goals

Central to the investment process is the establishment of clear and achievable financial goals that serve as guiding beacons for decision-making and resource allocation. Financial goals can vary widely depending on individual circumstances, aspirations, and timelines, but they generally fall into several broad categories, including short-term goals (e.g., saving for a vacation), medium-term goals (e.g., purchasing a home), and long-term goals (e.g., retirement planning). By articulating specific, measurable, attainable, relevant, and time-bound (SMART) goals, individuals can create a roadmap for their financial journey and prioritize their investment efforts accordingly.

Understanding Risk and Return

One of the fundamental principles of investing is the relationship between risk and return, wherein higher potential returns are typically associated with greater levels of risk. Risk refers to the uncertainty or volatility associated with an investment's potential returns, including the possibility of losing some or all of the invested capital. Different types of investments exhibit varying degrees of risk, with stocks generally considered more volatile than bonds, and alternative investments such as real estate or commodities carrying their own unique risk profiles.

Return, on the other hand, represents the financial gain or loss generated by an investment over a specified period. It can manifest in several forms, including capital appreciation, dividends, interest payments, or rental income. Investors seek to achieve a balance between risk and return that aligns with their financial goals, risk tolerance, and investment horizon. While higher-risk investments may offer the potential for greater returns, they also entail a higher likelihood of volatility and loss, underscoring the importance of diversification and risk management in building resilient investment portfolios.

Different Types of Investments

Investments come in various shapes and sizes, each offering its own unique characteristics, risk-reward profiles, and potential tax implications. Common types of investments include:

1. **Stocks**: Stocks represent ownership stakes in publicly traded companies and offer investors the potential for capital appreciation and dividends. They are typically more volatile than other asset classes but can provide superior returns over the long term.
2. **Bonds**: Bonds are debt securities issued by governments, municipalities, or corporations to raise capital. They offer fixed or variable interest payments, known as coupon payments, and return the principal amount upon maturity. Bonds are generally considered less risky than stocks but may offer lower returns.
3. **Mutual Funds**: Mutual funds pool money from multiple investors to invest in a diversified portfolio of stocks, bonds, or other assets. They offer professional management and diversification benefits but may charge fees and expenses.
4. **Exchange-Traded Funds (ETFs)**: ETFs are similar to mutual funds but trade on stock exchanges like individual stocks. They provide investors with exposure to a specific market index, sector, or asset class and offer liquidity and

low-cost diversification.

5. **Real Estate**: Real estate investments involve purchasing properties, such as residential homes, commercial buildings, or land, with the aim of generating rental income and capital appreciation. Real estate offers diversification benefits and inflation protection but requires ongoing maintenance and management.

6. **Commodities**: Commodities are physical goods, such as gold, oil, or agricultural products, that are traded on commodity exchanges. They serve as hedges against inflation and geopolitical risks but can be volatile and speculative in nature.

7. **Alternative Investments**: Alternative investments encompass a broad range of non-traditional assets, including hedge funds, private equity, venture capital, and cryptocurrency. They offer diversification benefits and the potential for high returns but often come with higher fees and liquidity constraints.

In summary, mastering the basics of investing entails setting clear financial goals, understanding the interplay between risk and return, and exploring the diverse universe of investment options available. By aligning investment decisions with their financial objectives, risk tolerance, and time horizon, individuals can construct well-balanced portfolios designed to weather market fluctuations and achieve long-term wealth accumulation.

2

Getting Started

Entering the realm of investing marks a significant milestone in one's financial journey, but it can also be overwhelming for those navigating the complexities of the financial markets for the first time. Getting started involves a multifaceted process that encompasses several key components, each of which plays a crucial role in shaping the trajectory of one's investment endeavors. From selecting the right brokerage account to conducting thorough research on potential investment opportunities and crafting a well-curated watchlist, the journey of getting started with investing is as much about education and preparation as it is about execution.

Opening a Brokerage Account

At the heart of the investment process lies the brokerage account, a vital tool that facilitates the buying and selling of securities in the financial markets. Opening a brokerage account is often the first step for aspiring investors, as it provides them with access to a wide range of investment products and trading services offered by brokerage firms. When selecting a brokerage account, individuals must consider a variety of factors, including fees and commissions, investment options, trading platforms, research tools, customer support, and regulatory compliance.

Choosing the right brokerage firm is paramount to the success of your investment journey, as it can significantly impact your trading experience and overall satisfaction. Some investors may opt for traditional full-service brokerage firms, which offer personalized investment advice and tailored portfolio management services but may charge higher fees. Others may prefer discount brokerage firms, which provide self-directed investing options at lower costs but may offer limited research tools and educational resources.

To open a brokerage account, individuals typically need to complete an application process that includes providing personal information, such as their name, address, Social Security number, employment status, and financial background. Additionally, they may be required to fund their account with an initial deposit, which can vary depending on the brokerage firm and the type of account being opened. Once the account is established, investors can begin exploring investment opportunities and executing trades based on their financial goals, risk tolerance, and investment horizon.

Researching Stocks

Researching stocks is an essential aspect of the investment process, as it enables investors to make informed decisions about which companies to invest in and when to buy or sell their shares. Stock research encompasses a broad range of methodologies and techniques, each aimed at evaluating the fundamental and technical attributes of individual companies and assessing their investment potential.

Fundamental analysis involves analyzing a company's financial statements, business model, industry dynamics, competitive position, management team, growth prospects, and valuation metrics to determine its intrinsic value and long-term investment attractiveness. Investors may examine key financial ratios, such as earnings per share (EPS), price-to-earnings (P/E) ratio, price-to-book (P/B) ratio, and return on equity (ROE), to assess a company's financial health and profitability relative to its peers.

Technical analysis, on the other hand, focuses on studying price charts, volume patterns, and market indicators to identify trends, patterns, and trading signals that may indicate future price movements. Technical analysts use various tools and techniques, such as moving averages, support and resistance levels, trendlines, and oscillators, to analyze historical price data and predict future price trends with a high degree of accuracy.

In addition to fundamental and technical analysis, investors may also consider qualitative factors, such as macroeconomic trends, industry developments, regulatory changes, geopolitical risks, and market sentiment, when researching stocks. By conducting thorough research and due diligence, investors can gain valuable insights into the companies they are considering investing in and make well-informed decisions that align with their investment objectives and risk tolerance.

Creating a Watchlist

Creating a watchlist is an integral part of the investment process, as it allows investors to monitor and track potential investment opportunities, stay informed about market developments, and identify trading opportunities in real-time. A watchlist is essentially a curated list of stocks that meet specific investment criteria or exhibit certain characteristics, such as strong earnings growth, attractive valuation metrics, or bullish technical patterns.

To create a watchlist, investors can leverage various tools and resources provided by brokerage firms, financial websites, and mobile apps. These tools often offer customizable features, such as real-time stock quotes, price alerts, news updates, research reports, and technical analysis charts, to help investors stay organized and informed about their investment options. Investors can add or remove stocks from their watchlist based on changing market conditions, new information, or evolving investment priorities.

In addition to monitoring individual stocks, investors may also use watchlists to track market indices, sector performance, economic indicators, and other relevant benchmarks that provide insights into broader market trends and sentiment. By regularly reviewing and updating their watchlists, investors can stay ahead of market developments, identify emerging opportunities, and adjust their investment strategies accordingly to capitalize on changing market dynamics.

In summary, getting started with investing involves a multifaceted process that encompasses several key components, including opening a brokerage account, researching stocks, and creating a watchlist. By taking these essential steps and leveraging the tools and resources available, investors can lay the foundation for a successful investment journey and work towards achieving their financial goals over time.

3

Understanding Market Fundamentals

Understanding market fundamentals is essential for investors seeking to navigate the complexities of the financial markets and make informed investment decisions. Market fundamentals encompass a broad range of factors that influence the behavior of financial markets, including supply and demand dynamics, economic conditions, corporate earnings, geopolitical events, and investor sentiment. By gaining a deeper understanding of market fundamentals, investors can better interpret market movements, identify potential opportunities and risks, and develop strategies to achieve their investment objectives.

One of the key components of market fundamentals is the concept of supply and demand. In financial markets, supply refers to the quantity of securities available for sale, while demand represents the desire of investors to purchase those securities. The interaction between supply and demand determines the price of securities, with prices rising when demand exceeds supply and falling when supply exceeds demand. Understanding supply and demand dynamics can help investors identify trends and patterns in the market and anticipate potential price movements.

Another important aspect of market fundamentals is economic conditions. Economic indicators, such as gross domestic product (GDP), inflation rates, unemployment rates, consumer spending, and industrial production, provide valuable insights into the health and direction of the economy. Positive economic indicators, such as strong GDP growth and low unemployment rates, are generally associated with bullish market conditions, while negative economic indicators may signal potential headwinds for the market. By monitoring economic indicators and their impact on market fundamentals, investors can adjust their investment strategies accordingly and position themselves for success in various market environments.

Corporate earnings are also a critical component of market fundamentals. Earnings reports, which companies release on a quarterly basis, provide detailed information about their financial performance, including revenue, profit margins, and earnings per share. Strong earnings growth is typically viewed positively by investors and can drive stock prices higher, while disappointing earnings results may lead to declines in stock prices. Understanding corporate earnings and their impact on market fundamentals can help investors identify high-quality companies with strong growth potential and avoid those with deteriorating financial prospects.

Investor sentiment is another factor that influences market

fundamentals. Investor sentiment refers to the overall mood or attitude of investors towards the market and can range from bullish optimism to bearish pessimism. Investor sentiment is often driven by a combination of factors, including economic conditions, corporate earnings, geopolitical events, and market trends. Positive investor sentiment can lead to buying activity and rising stock prices, while negative sentiment may result in selling pressure and declining stock prices. By gauging investor sentiment and its impact on market fundamentals, investors can better anticipate market trends and position themselves accordingly.

In summary, understanding market fundamentals is essential for investors seeking to navigate the complexities of the financial markets and achieve their investment objectives. By gaining insights into supply and demand dynamics, economic conditions, corporate earnings, and investor sentiment, investors can better interpret market movements, identify potential opportunities and risks, and develop strategies to capitalize on market trends.

Market Indexes and Averages

Market indexes and averages play a crucial role in providing investors with insights into the overall performance and direction of financial markets. These benchmarks track the performance of a specific group of stocks, bonds, or other securities and serve as reference points for comparing individual investments and measuring market trends. By understanding market indexes and averages, investors can gain valuable insights into market dynamics, track the performance of their investments, and make informed decisions about asset allocation and portfolio management.

One of the most widely recognized market indexes is the S&P 500, which tracks the performance of 500 large-cap U.S. companies and is often used as a benchmark for the broader U.S. stock market. The Dow Jones Industrial Average (DJIA), another popular market index, tracks the performance of 30 large-cap U.S. companies across various industries and is considered a barometer of the overall health of the U.S. economy. Other notable market indexes include the Nasdaq Composite, which tracks the performance of more than 2,500 U.S. and international stocks listed on the Nasdaq exchange, and the Russell 2000, which tracks the performance of 2,000 small-cap U.S. companies.

Market indexes are typically calculated using a weighted average methodology, where the relative weights of individual components are determined based on factors such as market capitalization, price, or equal weighting. For example, in a market-capitalization-weighted index like the S&P 500, larger companies with higher market capitalizations have a greater impact on the index's performance compared to smaller companies. In contrast, in an equal-weighted index, each component is assigned the same weight, regardless of its size or market capitalization.

In addition to market indexes, investors may also use moving averages to track the performance of financial markets and identify trends. Moving averages, which smooth out fluctuations in price data over a specific period, can help investors filter out noise and focus on the underlying trend of the market. Common types of moving averages include the simple moving average (SMA) and the exponential moving average (EMA), which calculate the average price of a security over a specified number of periods.

By monitoring market indexes and averages, investors can gain valuable insights into market trends, sentiment, and momentum, which can inform their investment decisions and help them navigate the complexities of the financial markets. Whether tracking the performance of a specific sector, asset class, or market segment, market indexes and averages serve as indispensable tools for investors seeking to achieve their investment objectives and maximize their returns.

Economic Indicators

Economic indicators play a crucial role in providing insights into the health and direction of the economy, influencing investor sentiment, market trends, and monetary policy decisions. These indicators, which encompass a wide range of data points and statistics, provide valuable information about the performance of key sectors of the economy, such as employment, consumer spending, manufacturing, housing, and inflation. By understanding economic indicators and their impact on financial markets, investors can gain valuable insights into market dynamics, make informed investment decisions, and position themselves for success in various market environments.

One of the most closely watched economic indicators is gross domestic product (GDP), which measures the total value of goods and services produced within a country's borders over a specific period, typically on a quarterly or annual basis. GDP growth is often used as a barometer of economic health, with strong GDP growth indicating robust economic activity and potential inflationary pressures, while weak GDP growth may signal economic downturns and potential deflationary risks. Investors closely monitor GDP reports and their implications for corporate earnings, interest rates, and monetary policy decisions.

Another important economic indicator is the unemployment rate, which measures the percentage of the labor force that is unemployed and actively seeking employment. Low unemployment rates are generally viewed positively by investors and may indicate a healthy labor market and potential wage growth, while high unemployment rates may signal economic weakness and potential challenges for consumer spending and corporate profitability. In addition to the headline unemployment rate, investors may also monitor other labor market indicators, such as jobless claims, labor force participation rates, and wage growth, to gain insights into labor market dynamics and trends.

Consumer spending is another key economic indicator that provides valuable insights into consumer confidence, household income, and overall economic activity. Consumer spending accounts for a significant portion of economic output in most countries and is influenced by factors such as employment levels, income growth, inflation, and consumer sentiment. Strong consumer spending is often associated with robust economic growth and may drive corporate earnings and stock prices higher, while weak consumer spending may indicate economic headwinds and potential challenges for businesses.

Housing market indicators, such as housing starts, home sales, and home prices, provide valuable insights into the health and direction of the housing market, which is a key driver of economic activity and consumer wealth. Rising home prices and strong housing market activity are generally viewed positively by investors and may signal economic expansion and potential wealth effects, while declining home prices and weak housing market activity may indicate economic contraction and potential challenges for consumer spending and economic growth.

Inflation indicators, such as the consumer price index (CPI) and the producer price index (PPI), measure changes in the prices of goods and services over time and provide insights into inflationary pressures and purchasing power. Moderate inflation is generally viewed positively by investors and may indicate healthy economic growth and rising demand, while high inflation rates may erode purchasing power and lead to higher interest rates and potential challenges for corporate profitability and consumer spending.

By understanding economic indicators and their implications for financial markets, investors can gain valuable insights into market dynamics, identify potential opportunities and risks, and make informed investment decisions that align with their investment objectives and risk tolerance. Whether monitoring GDP reports, employment data, consumer spending trends, or inflation indicators, economic indicators serve as indispensable tools for investors seeking to navigate the complexities of the financial markets and achieve their investment goals.

Reading Stock Quotes

Reading stock quotes is an essential skill for investors seeking to track the performance of individual stocks, assess market trends, and make informed investment decisions. Stock quotes provide valuable information about the current price, trading volume, and other key metrics of a particular stock, enabling investors to gauge its liquidity, volatility, and valuation relative to other stocks in the market. By understanding how to read and interpret stock quotes, investors can gain valuable insights into market dynamics, identify potential trading opportunities, and manage their investment portfolios more effectively.

A typical stock quote consists of several key elements, including:

1. **Ticker Symbol**: The ticker symbol is a unique alphabetic code assigned to each publicly traded company and serves as a shorthand identifier for the company's stock. Ticker symbols are typically composed of one to five letters and are used to look up stock quotes on financial websites,

trading platforms, and stock exchanges.

2. **Stock Price**: The stock price represents the current market price at which a share of the company's stock is trading. Stock prices are quoted in real-time and may fluctuate throughout the trading day based on supply and demand dynamics, market sentiment, and other factors.

3. **Bid and Ask Prices**: The bid price represents the highest price at which buyers are willing to purchase shares of the stock, while the ask price represents the lowest price at which sellers are willing to sell shares of the stock. The difference between the bid and ask prices is known as the bid-ask spread and reflects the liquidity and trading activity of the stock.

4. **Trading Volume**: Trading volume refers to the total number of shares of the stock that have been traded during a specified period, typically on a daily or weekly basis. Trading volume provides insights into the level of investor interest and activity in the stock and can help investors gauge liquidity and market sentiment.

5. **Previous Close**: The previous close represents the closing price of the stock on the previous trading day. It provides a reference point for investors to compare the current price of the stock and assess its performance relative to the previous trading session.

6. **Day's Range**: The day's range represents the range of prices at which the stock has traded during the current trading session, from the lowest price to the highest price. It provides insights into the intraday volatility and price movements of the stock and can help investors identify potential support and resistance levels.

7. **52-Week Range**: The 52-week range represents the range

of prices at which the stock has traded over the past 52 weeks, from the lowest price to the highest price. It provides insights into the stock's price history and volatility and can help investors assess its long-term performance and potential price targets.

8. **Market Cap**: Market capitalization, or market cap, represents the total market value of a company's outstanding shares of stock and is calculated by multiplying the current stock price by the total number of shares outstanding. Market cap provides insights into the size, scale, and valuation of the company relative to other companies in the market and is often used as a key metric for comparing stocks.

In addition to these key elements, stock quotes may also include other information, such as dividend yield, earnings per share (EPS), price-to-earnings (P/E) ratio, and other fundamental and technical metrics. By understanding how to read and interpret stock quotes, investors can gain valuable insights into market dynamics, track the performance of individual stocks, and make informed investment decisions that align with their investment objectives and risk tolerance.

In summary, reading stock quotes is an essential skill for investors seeking to track the performance of individual stocks, assess market trends, and make informed investment decisions. By understanding the key elements of a stock quote, investors can gain valuable insights into market dynamics, identify potential trading opportunities, and manage their investment portfolios more effectively. Whether monitoring stock prices, trading volume, bid-ask spreads, or other key metrics, reading stock quotes is an indispensable tool for investors seeking to navigate the complexities of the financial markets and achieve their investment goals.

4

Stock Market Strategies

Stock market strategies encompass a diverse range of approaches and techniques employed by investors to achieve their investment objectives and navigate the complexities of financial markets. These strategies are shaped by various factors, including investment goals, risk tolerance, time horizon, market conditions, and personal preferences. From long-term investing to short-term trading, value investing to growth investing, dividend investing to momentum trading, there are countless strategies available to investors seeking to capitalize on market opportunities and mitigate risks.

Long-Term vs. Short-Term Investing

One of the fundamental distinctions in stock market strategies is between long-term investing and short-term trading. Long-term investing involves buying and holding stocks for an extended period, typically several years or more, with the expectation of achieving capital appreciation and building wealth over time. Long-term investors focus on the underlying fundamentals of companies, such as earnings growth, competitive advantage, and management quality, and are less concerned with short-term market fluctuations.

In contrast, short-term trading involves buying and selling stocks within relatively short timeframes, ranging from minutes to days or weeks, with the goal of profiting from short-term price movements and market inefficiencies. Short-term traders often rely on technical analysis, market trends, and momentum indicators to identify trading opportunities and execute rapid-fire trades with the aim of generating quick profits. While short-term trading can be lucrative for skilled traders, it also carries higher risks and requires a significant time commitment and active management.

The choice between long-term investing and short-term trading depends on various factors, including investor objectives, risk tolerance, time horizon, and investment philosophy. Long-term investing is well-suited for investors seeking to build wealth gradually over time, take advantage of compound interest, and minimize transaction costs and taxes. Short-term trading, on the other hand, appeals to investors with a higher risk tolerance, shorter time horizons, and a penchant for active trading and market timing.

Value Investing

Value investing is a time-tested investment strategy pioneered by legendary investors such as Benjamin Graham and Warren Buffett, which involves identifying undervalued stocks trading below their intrinsic value and holding them for the long term. Value investors believe that markets are sometimes inefficient and that stocks can become mispriced due to temporary market fluctuations, investor sentiment, or other factors. By focusing on the underlying fundamentals of companies and buying stocks at a discount to their intrinsic value, value investors aim to achieve superior returns and minimize downside risk.

Key principles of value investing include:

- **Margin of Safety**: Value investors seek to buy stocks with a significant margin of safety, meaning they are trading at a discount to their intrinsic value, providing a buffer against potential downside risk.
- **Fundamental Analysis**: Value investors conduct thorough fundamental analysis of companies, examining factors such as earnings, cash flow, book value, dividends, competitive position, and management quality to assess their intrinsic value and investment potential.
- **Contrarian Approach**: Value investors often take a contrarian approach to investing, buying stocks that are out of favor or overlooked by the market but have strong fundamentals and long-term growth prospects.
- **Patience and Discipline**: Value investing requires patience and discipline, as stocks may take time to realize their full

23

value, and market sentiment may fluctuate in the short term. Value investors focus on the long-term outlook of companies and are willing to hold through market downturns and volatility.

Growth Investing

Growth investing is another popular investment strategy that focuses on identifying companies with strong growth potential and investing in them for the long term. Unlike value investing, which seeks to buy stocks at a discount to their intrinsic value, growth investing emphasizes investing in companies with above-average earnings growth rates, expanding market opportunities, and innovative products or services. Growth investors are willing to pay a premium for stocks with high growth prospects, betting on the company's ability to generate substantial returns over time.

Key principles of growth investing include:

- **Focus on Growth Potential**: Growth investors prioritize companies with strong growth potential, such as those operating in high-growth industries, with innovative business models, and scalable products or services.
- **Earnings Growth**: Growth investors look for companies with a track record of consistently growing earnings and revenue at an above-average rate compared to their peers and the broader market.

- **Quality Management**: Growth investors place a premium on strong management teams with a clear vision, disciplined execution, and a track record of delivering results. They believe that capable management is essential for driving long-term growth and creating shareholder value.
- **Tolerance for Volatility**: Growth investing involves investing in companies with high growth potential, which may be more volatile and susceptible to market fluctuations. Growth investors have a higher risk tolerance and are willing to endure short-term volatility in pursuit of long-term capital appreciation.

Dividend Investing

Dividend investing is a popular investment strategy that focuses on investing in companies that pay regular dividends to their shareholders. Dividends are cash payments made by companies to their shareholders out of their profits or retained earnings and are typically paid on a quarterly basis. Dividend investing appeals to investors seeking regular income, capital preservation, and long-term wealth accumulation, as dividends provide a steady stream of passive income and can help offset market volatility and inflationary pressures.

Key principles of dividend investing include:

- **Dividend Yield**: Dividend investors look for companies

with attractive dividend yields, which represent the annual dividend payment as a percentage of the stock price. Higher dividend yields indicate higher income potential for investors.

- **Dividend Growth**: Dividend investors also prioritize companies with a history of consistently increasing their dividends over time. Dividend growth companies demonstrate financial stability, strong cash flow generation, and a commitment to returning capital to shareholders.
- **Dividend Sustainability**: Dividend investors assess the sustainability of dividend payments by analyzing factors such as earnings growth, cash flow generation, payout ratios, and dividend coverage. They seek companies with a sustainable dividend policy that can weather economic downturns and market volatility.
- **Total Return**: Dividend investing focuses not only on dividend income but also on total return, which includes capital appreciation from stock price appreciation. Dividend investors aim to achieve a balance between current income and long-term capital appreciation to maximize total return over time.

In summary, stock market strategies encompass a diverse range of approaches and techniques employed by investors to achieve their investment objectives and navigate the complexities of financial markets. Whether pursuing long-term investing or short-term trading, value investing or growth investing, dividend investing or momentum trading, investors have a wide array of strategies at their disposal to capitalize on market opportunities and mitigate risks. By understanding the principles and strategies of stock market investing, investors can develop informed investment strategies that align with their goals, risk tolerance, and time horizon, and work towards achieving long-term financial success.

5

Building a Diversified Portfolio

Building a diversified portfolio is a fundamental principle of investing aimed at reducing risk and maximizing returns over the long term. A diversified portfolio consists of a mix of different asset classes, such as stocks, bonds, cash, and alternative investments, as well as a variety of investments within each asset class. The goal of diversification is to spread risk across multiple investments and asset classes, so that losses in one area of the portfolio may be offset by gains in another, thus minimizing the overall volatility of the portfolio and enhancing its stability.

Diversification can be achieved through several strategies, including:

1. **Asset Class Diversification**: Allocating investments across different asset classes, such as stocks, bonds, and cash, each of which has unique risk-return characteristics and behaves differently under various market conditions. For example, stocks tend to offer higher returns but also higher

volatility, while bonds provide income and stability but lower potential for capital appreciation.

2. **Sector Diversification**: Spreading investments across different sectors of the economy, such as technology, healthcare, consumer goods, and financial services, to reduce exposure to sector-specific risks and take advantage of diverse growth opportunities. Sector diversification helps mitigate the impact of adverse events that may affect specific industries or sectors.

3. **Geographic Diversification**: Investing in assets across different geographic regions and countries to reduce exposure to country-specific risks, political instability, currency fluctuations, and economic downturns. Geographic diversification allows investors to access global growth opportunities and benefit from the potential for diversification benefits across international markets.

4. **Company Size Diversification**: Allocating investments across companies of different sizes, such as large-cap, mid-cap, and small-cap stocks, to capture diverse opportunities across the market capitalization spectrum. Company size diversification helps mitigate concentration risk and provides exposure to companies at different stages of growth and development.

5. **Investment Style Diversification**: Diversifying across different investment styles, such as value investing, growth investing, and income investing, to take advantage of diverse investment strategies and market cycles. Investment style diversification helps balance risk and return objectives and adapt to changing market conditions.

By building a diversified portfolio, investors can reduce the overall risk of their investments while potentially increasing their returns over the long term. Diversification does not eliminate the risk of loss entirely, but it helps manage risk more effectively by spreading it across a range of investments with different risk-return profiles.

Asset Allocation

Asset allocation is the process of determining how to distribute investments across different asset classes within a portfolio based on an investor's financial goals, risk tolerance, investment horizon, and market outlook. Asset allocation is a critical component of portfolio construction, as it has a significant impact on both the risk and return characteristics of the portfolio. By strategically allocating investments across various asset classes, investors can optimize their portfolio's risk-return profile and enhance its potential for long-term growth and stability.

The key principles of asset allocation include:

1. **Strategic Asset Allocation**: Strategic asset allocation involves establishing a long-term target allocation to different asset classes based on an investor's financial goals, risk tolerance, and investment horizon. The strategic asset allocation serves as a roadmap for portfolio construction and provides a framework for making investment decisions over time.

2. **Asset Class Selection**: Asset allocation requires selecting the appropriate mix of asset classes, such as stocks, bonds, cash, and alternative investments, based on their risk-return characteristics and correlations with one another. The goal is to create a diversified portfolio that can withstand various market conditions and achieve consistent returns over time.

3. **Risk Management**: Asset allocation is a key tool for managing risk within a portfolio by diversifying across different asset classes with varying risk profiles. By spreading investments across assets that behave differently under different market conditions, investors can reduce the overall volatility of their portfolios and mitigate the impact of adverse events on their investment returns.

4. **Rebalancing**: Asset allocation requires periodic rebalancing to maintain the desired target allocation and ensure that the portfolio remains aligned with an investor's long-term goals and risk tolerance. Rebalancing involves buying or selling assets within the portfolio to bring its actual allocation back in line with the target allocation.

5. **Dynamic Asset Allocation**: Dynamic asset allocation involves adjusting the portfolio's asset allocation over time in response to changing market conditions, economic outlook, and investment opportunities. Dynamic asset allocation allows investors to take advantage of market trends and capitalize on emerging opportunities while managing downside risk.

Asset allocation is a dynamic process that requires regular review and adjustment to reflect changes in an investor's financial situation, market conditions, and investment objectives. By establishing a strategic asset allocation, selecting the appropriate mix of asset classes, and periodically rebalancing the portfolio, investors can optimize their investment returns and achieve their long-term financial goals.

Rebalancing Your Portfolio

Rebalancing your portfolio is a critical component of portfolio management aimed at maintaining the desired asset allocation and risk-return profile over time. Rebalancing involves periodically reviewing the composition of your portfolio, adjusting the allocation of assets, and realigning it with your long-term investment objectives and risk tolerance. By rebalancing your portfolio, you can mitigate the effects of market fluctuations, control risk, and ensure that your portfolio remains aligned with your financial goals.

The key principles of portfolio rebalancing include:

1. **Establishing a Rebalancing Strategy**: Rebalancing your portfolio begins with establishing a clear rebalancing strategy that outlines the frequency and threshold for rebalancing. Common rebalancing strategies include calendar-based rebalancing, where you rebalance your portfolio on a predetermined schedule, and threshold-based rebalancing, where you rebalance your portfolio when asset allocations deviate from their target levels by a certain percentage.
2. **Monitoring Asset Allocation**: Rebalancing your portfolio

requires monitoring the composition of your portfolio and tracking the allocation of assets relative to their target levels. Regularly review your portfolio's asset allocation and assess whether any adjustments are needed to bring it back in line with your target allocation.

3. **Adjusting Asset Allocation**: When rebalancing your portfolio, adjust the allocation of assets to bring it back in line with your target allocation. This may involve selling assets that have appreciated in value and reallocating the proceeds to assets that have underperformed or buying additional assets to increase exposure to underrepresented asset classes.

4. **Consideration of Taxes and Transaction Costs**: When rebalancing your portfolio, consider the tax implications and transaction costs associated with buying and selling assets. Minimize taxes and transaction costs by rebalancing in tax-efficient accounts, such as IRAs and 401(k)s, and using low-cost investment vehicles, such as index funds and ETFs.

5. **Rebalancing Frequency**: The frequency of portfolio rebalancing depends on various factors, including your investment goals, risk tolerance, and market conditions. Some investors rebalance their portfolios annually or semi-annually, while others rebalance more frequently or on an as-needed basis in response to significant market movements or changes in their financial situation.

Rebalancing your portfolio is a disciplined approach to portfolio management that helps maintain the desired asset allocation and risk-return profile over time. By periodically reviewing and adjusting your portfolio's asset allocation, you can control risk, optimize investment returns, and stay on track to achieve your long-term financial goals.

Risk Management

Risk management is a critical aspect of portfolio management aimed at identifying, assessing, and mitigating risks that may impact investment returns and portfolio performance. Effective risk management involves understanding the various types of risks that investors face, implementing strategies to manage and mitigate those risks, and monitoring the portfolio's risk exposure over time. By effectively managing risk, investors can protect their capital, preserve wealth, and achieve their long-term financial goals.

The key types of risks that investors face include:

1. **Market Risk**: Market risk, also known as systematic risk or undiversifiable risk, refers to the risk of losses due to broad market movements, such as changes in interest rates, economic conditions, geopolitical events, and investor sentiment. Market risk affects all investments to some degree and cannot be eliminated through diversification alone.

2. **Company-Specific Risk**: Company-specific risk, also known as idiosyncratic risk or diversifiable risk, refers to the risk of losses due to factors specific to individual companies, such as poor management, product recalls, competitive pressures, and regulatory changes. Company-

specific risk can be mitigated through diversification across different companies and industries.

3. **Credit Risk**: Credit risk, also known as default risk, refers to the risk of losses due to the inability of borrowers to repay their debts or obligations, such as bonds or loans. Credit risk is more prevalent in fixed-income investments, such as corporate bonds and high-yield bonds, and can be mitigated through credit analysis, diversification, and selecting high-quality issuers.

4. **Liquidity Risk**: Liquidity risk refers to the risk of losses due to the inability to buy or sell assets quickly and at a fair price without significantly impacting their market price. Illiquid investments, such as private equity, real estate, and certain bonds, may be more susceptible to liquidity risk, which can be mitigated through diversification and investing in liquid assets.

5. **Inflation Risk**: Inflation risk, also known as purchasing power risk, refers to the risk of losses due to the erosion of the real value of assets over time as a result of inflationary pressures. Inflation risk affects all investments to some extent and can be mitigated through investing in assets that offer inflation protection, such as stocks, real estate, and inflation-linked bonds.

Effective risk management involves implementing strategies to mitigate and control these risks, such as:

- **Diversification**: Diversifying across different asset classes, sectors, and geographic regions to spread risk and reduce exposure to any single risk factor or event.

- **Asset Allocation**: Allocating investments across different asset classes based on their risk-return characteristics and correlations to minimize overall portfolio risk.
- **Hedging**: Using derivative instruments, such as options, futures, and swaps, to hedge against specific risks, such as market volatility, interest rate fluctuations, and currency exposure.
- **Risk Assessment**: Regularly assessing and monitoring the portfolio's risk exposure using quantitative metrics, such as standard deviation, beta, and value at risk (VaR), and qualitative analysis of underlying risks and market conditions.
- **Stress Testing**: Conducting stress tests to assess the portfolio's resilience to adverse market scenarios and extreme events and adjusting risk management strategies accordingly.

By implementing these risk management strategies and continuously monitoring the portfolio's risk exposure, investors can protect their capital, preserve wealth, and achieve their long-term financial goals while minimizing the impact of market volatility and uncertainty. Effective risk management is an essential aspect of portfolio management that requires careful consideration and ongoing attention to ensure the portfolio remains resilient and well-positioned to navigate various market conditions and economic environments.

6

Executing Trades

Executing trades is a fundamental aspect of investing in financial markets, allowing investors to buy and sell securities such as stocks, bonds, options, and mutual funds. The execution of trades involves the process of transmitting orders to the market, matching buyers with sellers, and facilitating the exchange of securities at agreed-upon prices. Successful trade execution requires careful consideration of various factors, including market conditions, order types, execution strategies, and regulatory requirements. By understanding the mechanics of trade execution and employing effective trading strategies, investors can achieve their investment objectives and maximize their returns in the financial markets.

Market Orders vs. Limit Orders

Two primary types of orders commonly used by investors to execute trades in financial markets are market orders and limit orders.

1. **Market Orders**: A market order is an instruction to buy or sell a security at the best available market price. When a market order is placed, it is executed immediately at the prevailing market price, regardless of the price level. Market orders prioritize execution speed over price certainty, meaning that the exact price at which the trade is executed may vary from the quoted price at the time of order placement. Market orders are typically used when investors prioritize speed of execution and liquidity over price precision, such as in highly liquid markets or when trading large volumes of securities.

2. **Limit Orders**: A limit order is an instruction to buy or sell a security at a specified price or better. When a limit order is placed, it will only be executed if the market price reaches the specified limit price or better. Limit orders provide investors with greater control over the price at which their trades are executed, allowing them to specify a target price and avoid unfavorable price movements. Limit orders can be used to buy securities at a lower price than the current market price (buy limit order) or sell securities at a higher price than the current market price (sell limit order). Limit orders are commonly used when investors seek to achieve price certainty and minimize execution costs, such as in volatile markets or when trading illiquid securities.

Placing Buy and Sell Orders

Placing buy and sell orders involves specifying the quantity of securities to be bought or sold, the type of order (market or limit), and any additional instructions or conditions for the trade. Investors can place buy orders to purchase securities or sell orders to sell securities through various channels, including online brokerage platforms, trading apps, financial advisors, and traditional brokerage firms. When placing buy and sell orders, investors should consider factors such as the prevailing market conditions, order execution speed, liquidity of the security, trading costs, and investment objectives.

1. **Buy Orders**: When placing buy orders, investors specify the quantity of securities they wish to purchase, the type of order (market or limit), and the target price (for limit orders). Buy orders can be executed at the prevailing market price (market order) or at a specified price or better (limit order). Investors may also include additional instructions or conditions for the trade, such as time limits, order duration, or order contingencies.

2. **Sell Orders**: When placing sell orders, investors specify the quantity of securities they wish to sell, the type of order (market or limit), and the target price (for limit orders). Sell orders can be executed at the prevailing market price (market order) or at a specified price or better (limit order). Investors may also include additional instructions or conditions for the trade, such as stop-loss orders, trailing stop orders, or order contingencies.

Understanding Order Types

In addition to market orders and limit orders, there are several other types of orders that investors can use to execute trades in financial markets, each with its own unique characteristics and applications.

1. **Stop Orders**: A stop order, also known as a stop-loss order or stop-limit order, is an instruction to buy or sell a security once the market price reaches a specified price level, known as the stop price. Stop orders are used to limit losses or protect profits by triggering automatic buy or sell orders when the market moves in a certain direction. There are two types of stop orders: stop-market orders, which are executed at the prevailing market price once the stop price is reached, and stop-limit orders, which are executed at a specified price or better once the stop price is reached.

2. **Trailing Stop Orders**: A trailing stop order is a variation of a stop order that adjusts the stop price dynamically based on the market price of the security. Trailing stop orders are used to lock in profits or limit losses by automatically adjusting the stop price as the market price moves in a favorable direction. Trailing stop orders allow investors to capture gains while protecting against downside risk, as the stop price moves with the market price, maintaining a specified distance or percentage below the peak market price for long positions or above the trough market price for short positions.

3. **All-or-None Orders**: An all-or-none (AON) order is an instruction to execute the entire order quantity in a single

transaction or not at all. AON orders are used to ensure that the entire order is filled at once, rather than partially filled over multiple transactions, to avoid fragmented executions and maintain price integrity. AON orders are commonly used for large orders or illiquid securities, where partial fills may result in unfavorable execution prices or market impact.

4. **Fill or Kill Orders**: A fill or kill (FOK) order is an instruction to execute the entire order quantity immediately or cancel the order entirely. FOK orders are used to ensure that the entire order is filled in a single transaction without delay, and if it cannot be filled immediately, the order is canceled and not executed at all. FOK orders are commonly used for time-sensitive trades or when liquidity is limited, as they prioritize immediate execution over price considerations.

5. **Immediate or Cancel Orders**: An immediate or cancel (IOC) order is an instruction to execute the order immediately and fill whatever portion of the order can be executed, with any remaining unfilled portion canceled immediately. IOC orders are used to prioritize immediate execution over order completeness, allowing investors to capture available liquidity and minimize execution delays. IOC orders are commonly used for large orders or in fast-moving markets, where immediate execution is paramount.

By understanding the different types of orders available for executing trades in financial markets and their respective characteristics and applications, investors can effectively manage their portfolios, execute trades with precision, and achieve their investment objectives in various market conditions. Whether prioritizing execution speed, price certainty, or order completeness, investors can choose the order types that best align with their trading strategies, risk tolerance, and investment goals to optimize their trading performance and maximize their returns in the financial markets.

7

Evaluating Stocks

Evaluating stocks is a critical aspect of investing in the stock market, as it involves assessing the financial health, growth prospects, and valuation of individual companies to make informed investment decisions. There are various methods and tools available to evaluate stocks, including fundamental analysis, technical analysis, and the use of financial ratios. By conducting thorough stock evaluations, investors can identify attractive investment opportunities, mitigate risks, and build a well-rounded investment portfolio tailored to their investment objectives and risk tolerance.

Fundamental Analysis

Fundamental analysis is a method of evaluating stocks based on the analysis of a company's financial statements, business operations, industry trends, competitive position, and macroeconomic factors. The goal of fundamental analysis is to determine the intrinsic value of a stock and assess its potential for long-term growth and profitability. Fundamental analysts examine various quantitative and qualitative factors to assess the financial health and investment potential of a company, including:

1. **Financial Statements**: Fundamental analysts analyze a company's financial statements, including the income statement, balance sheet, and cash flow statement, to assess its revenue, expenses, assets, liabilities, and cash flow. They examine key financial metrics such as revenue growth, profit margins, return on equity (ROE), and free cash flow to gauge the company's financial performance and profitability.

2. **Business Operations**: Fundamental analysts evaluate a company's business operations, including its products or services, customer base, distribution channels, and competitive advantages, to assess its ability to generate sustainable revenue and earnings growth. They analyze industry trends, market dynamics, and competitive positioning to determine the company's competitive strengths and potential risks.

3. **Management Quality**: Fundamental analysts assess the quality of a company's management team, including its leadership, strategy, corporate governance practices, and track record of execution. They evaluate management's ability to allocate capital efficiently, innovate, adapt to changing market conditions, and create shareholder value over the long term.

4. **Industry Analysis**: Fundamental analysts conduct industry analysis to assess the company's position within

its industry, identify growth opportunities, and evaluate competitive threats. They analyze industry trends, regulatory environment, technological advancements, and competitive landscape to determine the company's growth potential and competitive advantages.

5. **Macroeconomic Factors**: Fundamental analysts consider macroeconomic factors such as interest rates, inflation, GDP growth, and geopolitical risks to assess the broader economic environment and its impact on the company's business operations, financial performance, and valuation. They analyze how macroeconomic trends and events may affect the company's revenue, expenses, profitability, and growth prospects.

By conducting thorough fundamental analysis, investors can gain valuable insights into the financial health, growth potential, and valuation of individual companies, allowing them to make informed investment decisions and identify attractive investment opportunities in the stock market.

Technical Analysis

Technical analysis is a method of evaluating stocks based on the analysis of historical price and volume data to identify patterns, trends, and trading signals that may indicate future price movements. Unlike fundamental analysis, which focuses on the intrinsic value of a stock and its underlying business fundamentals, technical analysis focuses solely on price action and market behavior. Technical analysts use various tools and techniques to analyze stock charts and identify potential buying or selling opportunities, including:

1. **Chart Patterns**: Technical analysts analyze stock charts to identify patterns and formations, such as support and resistance levels, trendlines, chart patterns (e.g., head and shoulders, double top/bottom), and candlestick patterns. These patterns are used to identify potential trend reversals, breakouts, and trading opportunities based on historical price movements and market psychology.

2. **Technical Indicators**: Technical analysts use a variety of technical indicators to analyze price and volume data and generate trading signals. Common technical indicators include moving averages, relative strength index (RSI), stochastic oscillator, MACD (moving average convergence divergence), Bollinger Bands, and volume indicators. These indicators are used to identify overbought or oversold conditions, trend strength, momentum, and potential trend reversals.

3. **Volume Analysis**: Technical analysts analyze trading volume to assess the strength and conviction behind price movements. High volume during price advances or declines may indicate strong buying or selling pressure, confirming the validity of price trends and signaling potential trading opportunities. Volume analysis helps technical analysts gauge market participation and assess the sustainability of price movements.

4. **Trend Analysis**: Technical analysts analyze price trends to identify the direction and strength of market trends. They use trendlines, moving averages, and trend-following

indicators to identify uptrends, downtrends, and sideways trends. Trend analysis helps technical analysts determine the overall market bias and position themselves accordingly to capitalize on trend continuation or reversal.

5. **Support and Resistance Levels**: Technical analysts identify support and resistance levels, which are price levels where buying or selling pressure is expected to emerge. Support levels represent areas where buying interest outweighs selling pressure, preventing further price declines, while resistance levels represent areas where selling pressure outweighs buying interest, preventing further price advances. Support and resistance levels help technical analysts identify potential entry and exit points and manage risk accordingly.

By employing technical analysis techniques, investors can gain insights into market sentiment, identify potential trading opportunities, and make more informed decisions about when to buy or sell stocks in the stock market. While technical analysis is primarily used by short-term traders and active investors, it can also complement fundamental analysis as part of a comprehensive investment strategy.

Using Financial Ratios

Financial ratios are quantitative measures used to assess the financial performance, profitability, liquidity, solvency, and valuation of individual companies. Financial ratios provide investors with valuable insights into a company's financial health and investment potential by comparing key financial metrics and benchmarking against industry peers and historical data. There are various categories of financial ratios used in stock analysis, including:

1. **Profitability Ratios**: Profitability ratios measure a company's ability to generate profits and returns for its shareholders. Common profitability ratios include return on equity (ROE), return on assets (ROA), gross profit margin, operating profit margin, and net profit margin. Profitability ratios help investors assess the efficiency of a company's operations and its ability to generate profits from its core business activities.

2. **Liquidity Ratios**: Liquidity ratios measure a company's ability to meet its short-term financial obligations and liquidity needs. Common liquidity ratios include the current ratio, quick ratio, and cash ratio. Liquidity ratios help investors assess the company's ability to cover its short-term liabilities and manage cash flow effectively.

3. **Solvency Ratios**: Solvency ratios measure a company's ability to meet its long-term financial obligations and debt repayment obligations. Common solvency ratios include the debt-to-equity ratio, debt-to-assets ratio, interest coverage ratio, and financial leverage ratio. Solvency ratios help investors assess the company's financial stability, leverage levels, and ability to withstand economic downturns or adverse market conditions.

4. **Efficiency Ratios**: Efficiency ratios measure a company's ability to use its assets and resources efficiently to generate revenue and profits. Common efficiency ratios include

asset turnover ratio, inventory turnover ratio, accounts receivable turnover ratio, and accounts payable turnover ratio. Efficiency ratios help investors assess the company's operational efficiency, asset utilization, and productivity levels.

5. **Valuation Ratios**: Valuation ratios measure a company's stock price relative to its earnings, book value, cash flow, and other financial metrics. Common valuation ratios include the price-to-earnings (P/E) ratio, price-to-book (P/B) ratio, price-to-sales (P/S) ratio, and price-to-cash flow (P/CF) ratio. Valuation ratios help investors assess the attractiveness of a company's stock price relative to its underlying fundamentals and compare it to industry peers and historical averages.

By analyzing financial ratios, investors can gain valuable insights into a company's financial health, performance, and valuation, allowing them to make more informed investment decisions and identify attractive investment opportunities in the stock market. Financial ratios provide a comprehensive framework for evaluating stocks and assessing their investment potential based on objective quantitative measures of financial performance and value. While financial ratios are not the sole determinant of a company's investment potential, they serve as valuable tools for conducting thorough stock analysis and making informed investment decisions in the stock market.

8

Risk Management and Psychology

Risk management and psychology play crucial roles in successful investing, as they influence decision-making, behavior, and outcomes in financial markets. Effective risk management involves identifying, assessing, and mitigating risks that may impact investment returns and portfolio performance, while understanding the psychological aspects of investing helps investors navigate emotions, biases, and cognitive errors that can lead to irrational decisions and poor investment outcomes. By integrating risk management principles with psychological insights, investors can enhance their decision-making processes, manage emotions effectively, and achieve long-term financial success in the stock market.

Risk management involves several key principles and strategies to mitigate risks and protect capital, including:

1. **Diversification**: Diversification is a fundamental risk management strategy that involves spreading investments across different asset classes, sectors, industries, and

geographic regions to reduce exposure to any single risk factor or event. Diversification helps mitigate the impact of market volatility, sector-specific risks, and company-specific risks, and enhances portfolio stability and resilience.

2. **Asset Allocation**: Asset allocation is the process of determining how to distribute investments across different asset classes, such as stocks, bonds, cash, and alternative investments, based on an investor's financial goals, risk tolerance, and investment horizon. Asset allocation helps balance risk and return objectives, optimize portfolio performance, and adapt to changing market conditions.

3. **Position Sizing**: Position sizing is the process of determining the appropriate size or weight of each investment position within a portfolio based on its risk-return characteristics, volatility, and correlation with other assets. By sizing positions appropriately, investors can manage risk exposure, limit potential losses, and maximize the efficiency of their portfolios.

4. **Stop-Loss Orders**: Stop-loss orders are risk management tools that automatically trigger the sale of a security once it reaches a predetermined price level, known as the stop price. Stop-loss orders help investors limit losses, protect capital, and manage downside risk by enforcing discipline and preventing emotional decision-making during periods of market volatility or adverse price movements.

Psychology plays a significant role in investor behavior and decision-making processes, influencing how individuals perceive, process, and respond to market information, uncertain-

ties, and risks. Common psychological factors that impact
investor behavior include:

1. **Emotions**: Emotions such as fear, greed, hope, and regret
   can cloud judgment, distort perception, and drive irrational
   decision-making in financial markets. Fear of losses may
   lead investors to panic sell during market downturns, while
   greed may lead to excessive risk-taking and overtrading.
   Managing emotions effectively is essential for maintaining discipline, staying focused on long-term goals, and
   avoiding impulsive decisions based on short-term market
   fluctuations.

2. **Biases**: Cognitive biases are inherent mental shortcuts
   and heuristics that influence perception, judgment, and
   decision-making processes. Common biases in investing include confirmation bias (seeking information that
   confirms existing beliefs), anchoring bias (relying too
   heavily on initial information or reference points), and
   overconfidence bias (overestimating one's abilities and
   underestimating risks). Recognizing and mitigating biases
   can help investors make more rational, evidence-based
   decisions and avoid common pitfalls.

3. **Herd Behavior**: Herd behavior refers to the tendency of
   individuals to follow the actions and behaviors of the
   crowd, rather than making independent decisions based
   on analysis and research. Herd behavior can lead to market
   bubbles, speculative frenzies, and excessive volatility,
   as investors react to perceived trends, momentum, and
   social influence rather than fundamental factors. Avoiding
   herd behavior and maintaining independent thinking are
   essential for making informed investment decisions and

avoiding undue influence from market sentiment.

4. **Loss Aversion**: Loss aversion is the tendency of individuals to prefer avoiding losses over acquiring gains, leading to risk-averse behavior and reluctance to take necessary risks to achieve long-term goals. Loss aversion can result in missed opportunities, underperformance, and suboptimal portfolio decisions, as investors prioritize preserving capital over maximizing returns. Overcoming loss aversion requires recognizing the importance of risk-taking, accepting temporary setbacks, and focusing on long-term objectives rather than short-term fluctuations.

Managing emotions and psychological biases is essential for effective risk management and investment success, as they can significantly impact decision-making processes, behavior, and outcomes in financial markets. By cultivating self-awareness, discipline, and emotional resilience, investors can navigate market uncertainties, overcome psychological barriers, and make rational, evidence-based decisions aligned with their long-term financial goals.

Managing Emotions

Managing emotions is crucial for successful investing, as emotions such as fear, greed, and anxiety can cloud judgment, distort perception, and lead to irrational decision-making in financial markets. Emotions influence how investors interpret market information, perceive risks, and respond to market fluctuations, often leading to impulsive actions, herd behavior, and suboptimal investment outcomes. By developing emotional intelligence, self-awareness, and coping strategies, investors can manage emotions effectively, maintain discipline, and make informed decisions aligned with their long-term financial goals.

1. **Self-Awareness**: Self-awareness is the ability to recognize and understand one's emotions, thoughts, and behaviors in response to market events and investment decisions. By cultivating self-awareness, investors can identify emotional triggers, biases, and patterns of behavior that may influence their decision-making processes. Self-awareness allows investors to pause, reflect, and respond thoughtfully rather than react impulsively to market fluctuations or perceived threats.

2. **Emotional Regulation**: Emotional regulation involves managing and controlling emotions effectively to avoid impulsive or irrational decisions in financial markets. Techniques such as deep breathing, mindfulness meditation, and visualization can help investors calm their minds, reduce stress, and regain emotional balance during periods of market volatility or uncertainty. Emotional regulation allows investors to make rational, evidence-based decisions based on analysis and research rather than succumbing to emotional impulses or knee-jerk reactions.

3. **Cognitive Restructuring**: Cognitive restructuring involves challenging and reframing irrational beliefs, cognitive distortions, and negative thought patterns that may contribute to emotional distress and poor decision-making in financial markets. By examining underlying assumptions, biases, and cognitive errors, investors can develop more

realistic and adaptive perspectives on market events, risks, and outcomes. Cognitive restructuring helps investors adopt a growth mindset, embrace uncertainty, and view setbacks as opportunities for learning and growth rather than sources of fear or anxiety.

4. **Stress Management**: Stress management techniques such as exercise, relaxation techniques, and time management can help investors reduce stress, improve resilience, and cope with the demands of investing in financial markets. Stress management allows investors to maintain focus, clarity, and composure during periods of market volatility or adversity, enabling them to make sound decisions and stay on course with their investment strategies. By prioritizing self-care and well-being, investors can enhance their emotional resilience and mental fortitude in navigating the ups and downs of the stock market.

5. **Seeking Support**: Seeking support from trusted mentors, financial advisors, or peer groups can provide investors with valuable guidance, perspective, and encouragement in managing emotions and navigating market challenges. By sharing experiences, insights, and strategies with others, investors can gain new perspectives, validate their feelings, and develop effective coping strategies for dealing with emotional ups and downs in financial markets. Seeking support fosters a sense of connection, community, and accountability, empowering investors to stay disciplined and resilient in pursuing their long-term financial goals.

Managing emotions effectively is essential for maintaining discipline, resilience, and clarity of thought in financial markets, as emotions can significantly influence decision-making processes and investment outcomes. By cultivating self-awareness, emotional regulation, and coping strategies, investors can navigate market uncertainties, overcome psychological barriers, and make informed decisions aligned with their long-term financial goals and objectives.

Avoiding Common Pitfalls

Avoiding common pitfalls is essential for successful investing, as certain behaviors, biases, and mistakes can undermine investment performance, erode wealth, and hinder progress towards long-term financial goals. By recognizing and avoiding common pitfalls, investors can enhance their decision-making processes, mitigate risks, and maximize their chances of achieving investment success in the stock market. Some of the most common pitfalls to avoid in investing include:

1. **Overtrading**: Overtrading occurs when investors buy and sell securities excessively, driven by impulsive decision-making, emotional trading, or a desire to time the market. Overtrading can result in high transaction costs, increased taxes, and suboptimal investment returns, as frequent trading erodes returns and reduces the benefits of compounding over time. Avoiding overtrading requires discipline, patience, and a focus on long-term investment objectives rather than short-term market fluctuations.

2. **Chasing Performance**: Chasing performance refers to the tendency of investors to buy securities or investment

strategies that have recently outperformed the market or peers, based on the belief that past performance will continue in the future. Chasing performance can lead to buying high and selling low, as investors chase momentum and trend-following strategies rather than focusing on underlying fundamentals and valuation. Avoiding chasing performance requires discipline, independent thinking, and a commitment to long-term investment principles rather than short-term fads or trends.

3. **Market Timing**: Market timing involves attempting to predict future market movements and selectively buying or selling securities based on short-term price forecasts or macroeconomic indicators. Market timing is notoriously difficult and unreliable, as it requires accurate predictions of market direction and timing, which is challenging to achieve consistently. Market timing strategies often lead to missed opportunities, increased trading costs, and underperformance relative to a buy-and-hold approach. Avoiding market timing requires a focus on long-term investing, diversification, and a disciplined investment strategy based on asset allocation and risk management.

4. **Ignoring Risk**: Ignoring risk involves overlooking or underestimating the potential risks and uncertainties associated with investing in financial markets. Risk is an inherent aspect of investing, and ignoring risk can lead to excessive risk-taking, overconcentration in high-risk assets, and unexpected losses during market downturns or adverse events. Avoiding risk requires a thorough understanding of the risks associated with each investment, diversification across different asset classes, and prudent risk management strategies, such as asset allocation, position sizing,

and stop-loss orders.

5. **Failing to Plan**: Failing to plan involves investing without a clear investment plan or strategy, leading to haphazard decision-making, inconsistent behavior, and suboptimal investment outcomes. A well-defined investment plan outlines specific goals, objectives, risk tolerance, and investment strategies tailored to an investor's financial situation and time horizon. Failing to plan can result in missed opportunities, inefficient portfolio management, and difficulty in tracking progress towards long-term goals. Avoiding this pitfall requires creating a comprehensive investment plan, regularly reviewing and updating it as needed, and adhering to a disciplined investment approach based on sound principles and practices.

By avoiding common pitfalls and adhering to sound investment principles and practices, investors can enhance their decision-making processes, mitigate risks, and increase their chances of achieving long-term investment success in the stock market. Avoiding overtrading, chasing performance, market timing, ignoring risk, and failing to plan requires discipline, patience, and a focus on long-term investment objectives rather than short-term market fluctuations or trends. By staying disciplined, focused, and committed to their investment strategies, investors can build wealth steadily over time and achieve their financial goals.

Setting Stop-Loss Orders

Setting stop-loss orders is a risk management strategy used by investors to limit potential losses, protect capital, and manage downside risk in financial markets. A stop-loss order is an instruction to sell a security once it reaches a predetermined price level, known as the stop price. Stop-loss orders help investors enforce discipline, avoid emotional decision-making, and minimize losses during periods of market volatility or adverse price movements. By setting stop-loss orders strategically, investors can mitigate downside risk, preserve capital, and stay on track with their long-term investment objectives.

1. **Determining Stop Price**: The first step in setting a stop-loss order is determining the appropriate stop price, which represents the price level at which the order will be triggered and the security will be sold. The stop price is typically set below the current market price for long positions and above the current market price for short positions, depending on the investor's risk tolerance, investment horizon, and trading strategy. Investors may base the stop price on technical analysis indicators, support and resistance levels, volatility measures, or percentage declines from entry prices.

2. **Setting Stop-Loss Order Type**: Once the stop price is determined, investors must choose the type of stop-loss order to use, based on their preferences and trading platform capabilities. Common types of stop-loss orders include:

- **Market Stop-Loss Order**: A market stop-loss order is

executed at the next available market price once the stop price is reached, regardless of the actual price at which the trade is executed. Market stop-loss orders prioritize execution speed over price certainty and guarantee that the trade will be executed promptly once the stop price is triggered.

- **Stop-Limit Order**: A stop-limit order is executed at a specified price or better once the stop price is reached, ensuring that the trade is executed at or near the desired price level. Stop-limit orders provide investors with greater control over the price at which their trades are executed but may risk partial or non-execution if the market price moves quickly through the specified limit price.

1. **Considering Volatility and Liquidity**: When setting stop-loss orders, investors should consider the volatility and liquidity of the security, as well as market conditions and trading volumes. Highly volatile or illiquid securities may experience rapid price movements or gaps, making it challenging to execute stop-loss orders at desired price levels. In such cases, investors may need to adjust stop-loss orders accordingly or use alternative risk management strategies to mitigate downside risk effectively.

2. **Monitoring and Adjusting Stop-Loss Orders**: Once stop-loss orders are set, investors should monitor market developments, news events, and price movements to assess whether adjustments to stop-loss levels are warranted. In fast-moving markets or volatile conditions, stop-loss orders may need to be adjusted to reflect changes in risk profiles, support and resistance levels, or technical indicators. Regularly reviewing and adjusting stop-loss orders

allows investors to adapt to changing market conditions and protect their capital effectively.

3. **Avoiding Emotional Decision-Making**: Stop-loss orders help investors avoid emotional decision-making and prevent impulsive reactions to market fluctuations or adverse price movements. By setting predetermined stop-loss levels and sticking to their trading plans, investors can maintain discipline, stay focused on long-term objectives, and avoid the psychological pitfalls of fear, greed, and regret that can lead to irrational decisions and poor investment outcomes.

Setting stop-loss orders is a critical risk management strategy that helps investors limit losses, protect capital, and manage downside risk effectively in financial markets. By determining appropriate stop prices, selecting the appropriate type of stop-loss order, considering volatility and liquidity factors, monitoring market developments, and avoiding emotional decision-making, investors can enhance their risk management practices, preserve capital, and stay on track with their investment objectives in the stock market. Whether used for short-term trading or long-term investing, stop-loss orders are valuable tools for protecting against adverse market movements and ensuring prudent portfolio management in various market conditions.

9

The Future of Investing

The future of investing is being shaped by technological advance-ments, demographic shifts, regulatory changes, and evolving market dynamics, creating new opportunities and challenges for investors worldwide. As technology continues to revolutionize financial markets, investors are embracing innovative solutions such as robo-advisors, algorithmic trading, and digital assets to optimize portfolio management, enhance decision-making pro-cesses, and access new investment opportunities. Additionally, demographic trends such as population growth, urbanization, and aging populations are driving demand for sustainable investing, impact investing, and socially responsible investing (SRI), as investors seek to align their financial goals with environmental, social, and governance (ESG) considerations. Regulatory changes and policy developments are also shaping the future of investing, with governments around the world implementing reforms to promote transparency, stability, and investor protection in financial markets.

1. **Technological Advancements**: Technological innovations

are transforming the investment landscape, enabling investors to access financial markets, research investment
opportunities, and execute trades more efficiently and
cost-effectively than ever before. Advances in artificial
intelligence (AI), machine learning, and big data analytics
are revolutionizing investment research and decision-
making processes, empowering investors to analyze vast
amounts of data, identify market trends, and generate
actionable insights in real time. Robo-advisors, which
use algorithms to automate portfolio management and
asset allocation, are gaining popularity among investors
seeking low-cost, passive investment solutions tailored to
their risk tolerance and financial goals. Blockchain technology and cryptocurrencies are also disrupting traditional
finance, offering investors new ways to invest, transact,
and store value in decentralized digital assets.

2. **Demographic Shifts**: Demographic trends such as population growth, urbanization, and aging populations are influencing investment preferences and strategies, as investors
adapt to changing consumer behavior, market demand,
and economic conditions. Millennials and Generation Z,
who grew up in the digital age, are driving demand for
technology-enabled investment solutions, socially responsible investing, and impact investing, as they prioritize
sustainability, transparency, and ethical considerations
in their investment decisions. Aging populations and
retirement demographics are fueling demand for income-
generating investments, retirement planning solutions,
and long-term care services, as investors seek to secure
their financial futures and mitigate longevity risks.

3. **Regulatory Changes**: Regulatory reforms and policy de-

velopments are reshaping the regulatory landscape for investors, asset managers, and financial institutions, as governments seek to promote transparency, stability, and investor protection in financial markets. Regulatory initiatives such as the Markets in Financial Instruments Directive (MiFID II), the General Data Protection Regulation (GDPR), and the Dodd-Frank Wall Street Reform and Consumer Protection Act are imposing stricter reporting requirements, transparency standards, and compliance obligations on market participants, enhancing market integrity and reducing systemic risks. Environmental, social, and governance (ESG) considerations are also gaining prominence in regulatory frameworks, with regulators encouraging companies to disclose non-financial information, adopt sustainable business practices, and address social and environmental risks.

4. **Market Dynamics**: Evolving market dynamics, including globalization, geopolitical risks, and macroeconomic trends, are influencing investment strategies and asset allocation decisions, as investors seek to navigate uncertainty, manage risks, and capitalize on emerging opportunities in global markets. Geopolitical tensions, trade disputes, and geopolitical events such as Brexit and the COVID-19 pandemic are creating volatility and uncertainty in financial markets, impacting asset prices, investor sentiment, and market correlations. Economic trends such as low interest rates, inflationary pressures, and central bank policies are driving demand for alternative investments, real assets, and inflation-hedging strategies, as investors seek to preserve purchasing power and generate returns in a low-yield environment.

The future of investing is characterized by innovation, adaptation, and disruption, as investors embrace technological advancements, demographic shifts, regulatory changes, and evolving market dynamics to achieve their financial goals and objectives. By staying informed, agile, and forward-thinking, investors can capitalize on emerging trends, identify attractive investment opportunities, and navigate market uncertainties effectively in an ever-changing investment landscape.

Exploring Other Investment Opportunities

Exploring other investment opportunities beyond traditional stocks and bonds can diversify portfolios, enhance returns, and mitigate risks, as investors seek to capitalize on emerging trends, disruptive technologies, and alternative asset classes. While stocks and bonds remain fundamental components of diversified investment portfolios, other investment opportunities such as real estate, private equity, venture capital, commodities, and digital assets offer unique benefits and opportunities for investors to generate alpha, achieve portfolio diversification, and hedge against inflationary risks.

1. **Real Estate**: Real estate investments, including residential properties, commercial properties, and real estate investment trusts (REITs), offer investors the opportunity to generate rental income, benefit from property appreciation, and diversify their investment portfolios with tangible assets. Real estate investments provide income stability,

inflation protection, and portfolio diversification benefits, as they tend to have low correlation with traditional asset classes such as stocks and bonds. Real estate crowdfunding platforms and real estate investment platforms enable investors to access real estate investments with lower capital requirements, reduced barriers to entry, and enhanced liquidity compared to direct property ownership.

2. **Private Equity**: Private equity investments involve investing in privately held companies or private equity funds that acquire, operate, and grow businesses with the potential for long-term value creation and capital appreciation. Private equity investments offer investors the opportunity to access high-growth companies, participate in entrepreneurial ventures, and achieve attractive risk-adjusted returns that are uncorrelated with public market indices. Private equity funds provide diversification benefits, downside protection, and access to specialized investment strategies, such as leveraged buyouts, growth equity, and venture capital, which are not available in public markets.

3. **Venture Capital**: Venture capital investments involve investing in early-stage or growth-stage companies with high growth potential, disruptive technologies, and innovative business models that have the potential to generate outsized returns over the long term. Venture capital investments offer investors the opportunity to participate in the innovation economy, support entrepreneurial ventures, and capitalize on emerging trends in technology, healthcare, and other industries. Venture capital funds provide access to a diversified portfolio of startups, access to experienced investment managers, and exposure to

potential unicorns and IPO opportunities that can generate significant wealth creation.

4. **Commodities**: Commodities investments involve investing in physical commodities such as gold, silver, oil, natural gas, agricultural products, and precious metals, as well as commodity futures contracts and exchange-traded funds (ETFs) that track commodity prices. Commodities investments offer investors diversification benefits, inflation protection, and portfolio hedging capabilities, as they tend to have low correlation with traditional asset classes such as stocks and bonds. Commodities provide a hedge against inflationary risks, currency depreciation, and geopolitical uncertainties, as they serve as tangible assets with intrinsic value and global demand.

5. **Digital Assets**: Digital assets investments involve investing in cryptocurrencies, blockchain technology, and digital platforms that enable decentralized finance (DeFi), non-fungible tokens (NFTs), and digital securities. Digital assets offer investors exposure to emerging technologies, decentralized ecosystems, and alternative investment opportunities that are transforming finance, commerce, and digital ownership. Cryptocurrencies such as Bitcoin and Ethereum provide diversification benefits, inflation protection, and potential for capital appreciation, as they serve as store of value assets and alternative forms of money in the digital age.

Exploring other investment opportunities beyond traditional stocks and bonds can enhance portfolio diversification, reduce risk, and optimize returns for investors seeking to capitalize on emerging trends, disruptive technologies, and alternative asset classes. By incorporating real estate, private equity, venture capital, commodities, and digital assets into their investment portfolios, investors can access unique opportunities for alpha generation, portfolio hedging, and long-term wealth creation in a dynamic and evolving investment landscape

.

Continuing Your Education

Continuing your education as an investor is essential for staying informed, adapting to changing market conditions, and achieving long-term investment success in financial markets. By pursuing ongoing education and professional development opportunities, investors can enhance their knowledge, skills, and expertise in investment analysis, portfolio management, and financial planning, enabling them to make informed decisions, manage risks effectively, and achieve their financial goals and objectives. Whether through self-directed learning, formal education programs, or professional certifications, continuing education empowers investors to stay ahead of the curve, navigate market uncertainties, and capitalize on emerging opportunities in the stock market.

1. **Self-Directed Learning**: Self-directed learning involves taking initiative to acquire new knowledge, skills, and insights through independent study, research, and exploration of investment topics and strategies. Self-directed learners leverage a variety of educational resources, including books, articles, websites, podcasts, webinars, and

68

online courses, to deepen their understanding of financial markets, investment principles, and portfolio management techniques. Self-directed learning allows investors to tailor their education to their specific interests, preferences, and learning styles, enabling them to build expertise and confidence in managing their investment portfolios effectively.

2. **Formal Education Programs**: Formal education programs, such as undergraduate or graduate degrees in finance, economics, or business administration, provide investors with structured curriculum, academic rigor, and faculty expertise to develop a comprehensive understanding of financial markets, investment theories, and quantitative analysis techniques. Formal education programs offer investors a solid foundation in finance and investment principles, as well as opportunities for networking, mentorship, and career advancement in the finance industry. Whether pursuing a degree full-time or part-time, formal education programs equip investors with analytical skills, critical thinking abilities, and decision-making frameworks to succeed in dynamic and competitive financial markets.

3. **Professional Certifications**: Professional certifications, such as the Chartered Financial Analyst (CFA), Certified Financial Planner (CFP), and Chartered Alternative Investment Analyst (CAIA) designations, demonstrate proficiency, competence, and ethical conduct in specific areas of finance and investment management. Professional certifications provide investors with specialized knowledge, industry recognition, and credibility to enhance their career prospects, expand their professional networks, and differentiate themselves in the marketplace. By obtaining

professional certifications, investors signal their commitment to continuous learning, professional excellence, and ethical standards, positioning themselves as trusted advisors and subject matter experts in their field.

4. **Industry Conferences and Seminars**: Industry conferences, seminars, and workshops offer investors valuable opportunities to stay updated on industry trends, best practices, and emerging technologies in financial markets. Industry events bring together thought leaders, industry experts, and practitioners to share insights, exchange ideas, and discuss current issues and challenges facing investors and financial professionals. Attending industry conferences and seminars enables investors to network with peers, gain new perspectives, and access cutting-edge research and thought leadership in finance and investment management.

5. **Online Learning Platforms**: Online learning platforms, such as Coursera, Udemy, and LinkedIn Learning, offer investors a wide range of online courses, tutorials, and educational resources on finance, investment, and related topics. Online learning platforms provide flexibility, accessibility, and convenience for investors to acquire new skills, learn at their own pace, and access high-quality educational content from leading instructors and institutions around the world. Whether seeking to learn the basics of investing or advanced topics in portfolio management, online learning platforms offer investors a wealth of educational opportunities to enhance their knowledge and expertise in financial markets.

Continuing your education as an investor is a lifelong journey of learning, growth, and self-improvement, as you seek to stay informed, adapt to changing market conditions, and achieve your financial goals and objectives in an increasingly complex and dynamic investment landscape. By investing in your education and professional development, you empower yourself to make informed decisions, manage risks effectively, and build wealth steadily over time, ensuring long-term financial success and prosperity.

Becoming a Lifelong Investor

Becoming a lifelong investor is a commitment to continuous learning, self-improvement, and disciplined investing practices that empower individuals to achieve their financial goals and objectives over the long term. Lifelong investors embrace a mindset of curiosity, adaptability, and resilience as they navigate market uncertainties, overcome challenges, and capitalize on opportunities in financial markets. By adopting a holistic approach to investing that incorporates education, diversification, and disciplined portfolio management, lifelong investors can build wealth steadily over time, preserve purchasing power, and achieve financial independence and security for themselves and future generations.

1. **Commitment to Education**: Lifelong investors prioritize education and continuous learning as foundational pillars of their investment philosophy, recognizing that knowledge is the key to making informed decisions, managing

risks effectively, and achieving long-term investment success. Lifelong investors pursue ongoing education through self-directed learning, formal education programs, professional certifications, and industry conferences to deepen their understanding of financial markets, investment principles, and portfolio management techniques. By investing in their education, lifelong investors equip themselves with the knowledge, skills, and expertise to navigate market uncertainties, capitalize on emerging opportunities, and achieve their financial goals and objectives over time.

2. **Embrace Diversification**: Lifelong investors embrace diversification as a core principle of portfolio management, recognizing that spreading investments across different asset classes, sectors, and geographic regions can reduce risk, enhance returns, and improve the overall risk-return profile of their investment portfolios. Lifelong investors allocate assets strategically based on their risk tolerance, investment horizon, and financial goals, diversifying across stocks, bonds, real estate, commodities, and alternative investments to mitigate concentration risk and optimize portfolio performance. By embracing diversification, lifelong investors can weather market fluctuations, preserve capital, and achieve long-term investment success through prudent risk management and asset allocation strategies.

3. **Disciplined Portfolio Management**: Lifelong investors practice disciplined portfolio management, adhering to a well-defined investment plan, asset allocation strategy, and rebalancing schedule to maintain portfolio integrity, minimize behavioral biases, and stay focused on long-term objectives. Lifelong investors set clear investment goals,

establish realistic expectations, and monitor portfolio performance regularly to track progress towards their financial goals and adjust their investment strategies as needed. By maintaining discipline, patience, and consistency in their investment approach, lifelong investors can withstand market volatility, avoid emotional decision-making, and achieve sustainable wealth accumulation over time.

4. **Adaptability and Resilience**: Lifelong investors demonstrate adaptability and resilience in navigating market uncertainties, overcoming setbacks, and capitalizing on opportunities in financial markets. Lifelong investors recognize that market conditions are constantly evolving and that the ability to adapt to changing circumstances, embrace innovation, and capitalize on emerging trends is essential for long-term investment success. By maintaining a flexible mindset, embracing change, and learning from both successes and failures, lifelong investors can navigate market cycles, seize investment opportunities, and achieve their financial goals and objectives over the course of their investment journey.

5. **Focus on Long-Term Value Creation**: Lifelong investors focus on long-term value creation and wealth preservation, prioritizing sustainable growth, compounding returns, and wealth accumulation over time. Lifelong investors take a patient, disciplined approach to investing, avoiding short-term speculation, market timing, and chasing fads or trends in favor of sound investment principles and practices that have stood the test of time. By focusing on long-term value creation, rather than short-term fluctuations or market noise, lifelong investors can build wealth steadily

over time, achieve financial independence, and leave a lasting legacy for themselves and future generations.

Becoming a lifelong investor is a journey of self-discovery, growth, and empowerment as you pursue your financial goals and aspirations over the course of your life. By embracing education, diversification, disciplined portfolio management, adaptability, and a focus on long-term value creation, lifelong investors can navigate market uncertainties, overcome challenges, and achieve financial independence and security for themselves and future generations. As you embark on your journey as a lifelong investor, remember that patience, discipline, and perseverance are the keys to long-term investment success in an ever-changing and unpredictable world.

10

Conclusion

In conclusion, delving into the realm of stock market trading for teens signifies an expedition toward financial literacy, independence, and beyond—a journey ripe with opportunities for personal growth, learning, and empowerment. This venture isn't merely about the pursuit of wealth accumulation; it's about equipping teens with the tools, knowledge, and mindset to navigate the complexities of financial markets and make informed decisions that resonate throughout their lives.

Embarking on stock market trading at a young age provides teens with a unique platform to cultivate essential life skills, such as critical thinking, decision-making, and risk management. Through firsthand experience in analyzing stocks, tracking market trends, and executing trades, teens develop a deep understanding of the intricacies of investing—an invaluable asset that transcends financial realms and extends into various facets of their personal and professional lives.

Moreover, engaging in stock market trading fosters a culture of responsibility, resilience, and long-term value creation among teens. As they navigate the ebbs and flows of market dynamics, encountering both successes and setbacks, teens learn to adapt to uncertainty, persevere through challenges, and remain steadfast in pursuit of their financial goals. They come to appreciate the significance of discipline, patience, and strategic planning in achieving sustainable wealth accumulation—a lesson that reverberates far beyond the confines of the trading floor.

Furthermore, stock market trading serves as a catalyst for self-discovery and exploration, empowering teens to uncover their strengths, passions, and aspirations. As they immerse themselves in the world of investing, teens gain insight into their risk tolerance, investment preferences, and long-term objectives, laying the groundwork for informed decision-making and intentional wealth management.

In essence, stock market trading for teens transcends mere financial transactions; it embodies a transformative journey of personal growth, empowerment, and lifelong learning. By embracing the opportunities and challenges presented by the stock market with curiosity, diligence, and integrity, teens not only pave the way toward financial success but also cultivate a mindset of resilience, adaptability, and ambition that propels them toward a future filled with boundless possibilities. As they embark on this journey, may they remember that the true value of investing lies not solely in the returns it yields but in the knowledge, experience, and wisdom it bestows upon them—an invaluable legacy that endures for generations to come.

www.ingramcontent.com/pod-product-compliance
Lightning Source LLC
Chambersburg PA
CBHW071100290526

45795CB00004B/1595